Sebi the Colt

I'm rich in love Grandma.
Kelley

For my beautiful Ravann and to the pure joy of Sebastian, "Sebi."

My love for you is never ending. Until we hug again, to the right, so our hearts can touch once more.

One love,
Mom and Grandmas

#ravannandsebi4ever

Hi. I'm Sebastian.
But my friends call me Sebi for short.

I was born a few months ago
in the Outer Banks of North Carolina,
and spend my days on the beach
with my mom.

Oh and by the way, I am a Mustang colt, and my mom, she's a black raven.

How is that possible you ask?
Well before I was a horse,
                I was a human boy,
and my mom...
                she was a human too.
A beautiful woman with big dark eyes,
and long black hair.
I have her eyes, and hers are like
her mothers.

We were always together she and I, even when we left the world as humans and came back.

I **love** my new colt body!

I remember visiting the herds of horses when I was a human. We would drive onto the beach and watch them run along the shore. I always wondered what it would be like to gallop along the edge of the ocean as fast as I could go.

It's more fun than I ever imagined!

My mother, now in her raven body, caws to me from behind the dunes as we play a game of hide and seek!

Even though she could easily find me, she doesn't fly too high so I can always find a good hiding spot.

When it's my turn to seek, she likes to fly from behind me and return quickly to her spot before I can catch her!

At night under the light of the moon and stars, we walk along the shore.

Well, I walk

she hops, and flies, and sometimes I carry her on my back

WHICH IS FUN

because I couldn't do that when we were humans.

Another night not long ago
the ocean water was glowing
a **greenish blue** color!

Mom told me it was called

b i o l u m i n e s c e n c e.

She's one smart lady!

Often we talk about
>   our past lives as humans.
We had many friends,
>   and **the best** family!

Sometimes my grandmas
>   and our other human friends
come to check on us
>   and it feels so good to see them.

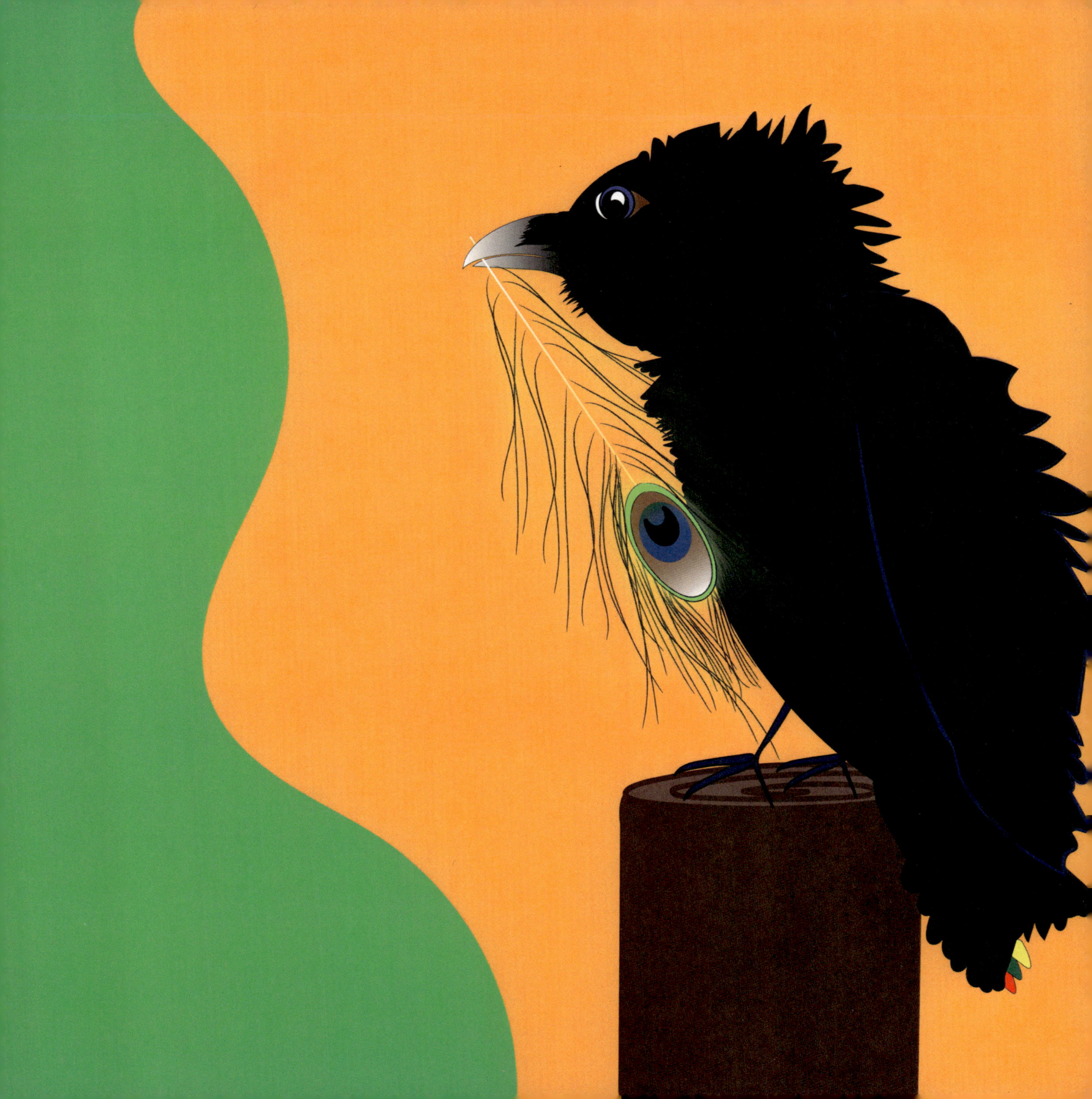

Life sure can be beautiful,
    and sad all at the same time.

But in the end
    if we add up all of the good stuff
it would s t r e t c h
    as far as the horizon
    and **beyond**.

Then the sad stuff would wash away
in the surf
like my hoof prints, and
mom's funny tracks
she leaves behind in the sand.

Well it's almost dark
and the sun is setting.

I can tell
it's going to be a
good one tonight.

I hope my family is watching it too.

As soon as it's dark I am going to see if mom wants to join me in a ghost crab hunt.

She's great at scaring them away before I accidentally step on one, and I'm great at finding the **big** ones!

I wonder what it would be like to be one.

Maybe one day I'll know!

Until then
I am having fun as a mustang,
and I'm pretty sure mom is happy being a raven.
She can keep an eye on me much easier this way
and I don't mind one bit,

unless it's my turn to hide!

The End

...or is it?

Did you find all the peacock feathers inside the book? Here's what they mean:

Peacock Feather

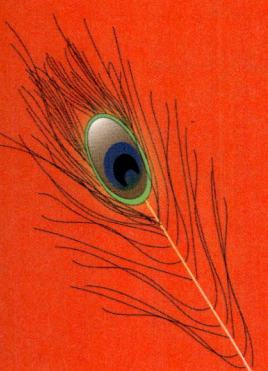

It has long been believed that anyone who wears a peacock feather would be protected from bad happenings. The beautiful iridescence and it's colors represent the rays of the sun as it rises on a new day. If you have ever seen a peacock fan his tail feathers as it struts to and fro, you can see why their feathers not only symbolize immortality, but also the power of positivity and pride.

Ravann proudly wore a tattoo of a peacock feather across her back and right shoulder. She believed what it sumbolized and there is no doubt she is eternally protected from harm in her next life.

> **Fun fact:** Did you know that Peacocks eat poisoniness plants with no ill side effects?

Did you notice the Red, Yellow, and Green colors?

Rasta Colors

Ravann lived a life heavily influenced by music. Her RAVRA music production business brought her community "**music & events that move you**".

She believed in unniversal music full of rhythm that made everyone move no matter who we are...or who we love. Her mantra was "One Love", made popular by the famous song by raggae artist Bob Marley, a proclaimed rastafarian.

The sun rose and blessed Kelley Grider Horton with her daughter Ravann Rachelle in Vancouver, Washington on September 6, 1980. When the sun rose on November 6, 2010, Ravann was gifted with Sebastian (Sebi) Antonio Lopez, in Nags Head, North Carolina.

On May 17, 2020 they enjoyed their last sunset together over the beautiful sand and waves of the Outer Banks of North Carolina.

Ravann was a kind, caring, and beautiful person, with a heart that was larger than life. She was always up for the cause, doing fundraisers and helping those in need in her beautiful Outer Banks community.

The peek-a-boo wall mural at Dowdy Park created by friend's Amylynn McCabe, Fay Davis Edwards & Dawn Gray Moraga.

Ravann was the founder of RAVRA Productions, bringing highly sought after raggae bands to the Outer Banks, including The Wailers, EarthKry, Steel Pulse, and The Movement. Her contributions and volunteer work with Dowdy Park in Nags Head, NC and the Artrageous Kids Art Festival held there annually, will live on as the event continues each year. Vistors to the park can pay their respects at the Peek-a-Boo wall now covered in a beautiful mural dedicated to Ravann and Sebi by artist friends, and family.

Sebastian was a perfect mix of all that is good. He was caring, kind, and respected Mother Earth with a deep love for animals. On a horse tour in Corolla early in 2019, Sebi and his mother had the pleasure of meeting the soon to be parents of the Mustang colt who was born just a few weeks after Sebi and his mother perished in a tragic house fire.

The Corolla Wild Horse Fund board unanimously chose to name the newborn colt after Sebastian.

Anyone who knew him, knew his love for life and for his family. He loved music and enjoyed being his mom's right-hand man. It was rare you ever saw mother without son. They were inseparable. It was only fitting then, that The Higher Power decided they leave this earth together.

Made in the USA
Middletown, DE
10 April 2021